AMAZING INVENTIONS

CAMERA

WITHDRAWN

MARY ELIZABETH SALZMANN

Consulting Editor, Diane Craig, M.A./Reading Specialist

Sandcastle

An Imprint of Abdo Publishing
abdopublishing.com

abdopublishing.com

Published by Abdo Publishing, a division of ABDO, PO Box 398166, Minneapolis, Minnesota 55439. Copyright © 2016 by Abdo Consulting Group, Inc. International copyrights reserved in all countries. No part of this book may be reproduced in any form without written permission from the publisher. SandCastle™ is a trademark and logo of Abdo Publishing.

Printed in the United States of America, North Mankato, Minnesota

062015
092015

Editor: Alex Kuskowski
Content Developer: Nancy Tuminelly
Cover and Interior Design and Production: Mighty Media, Inc.
Photo Credits: Library of Congress, Shutterstock, Wikimedia

Library of Congress Cataloging-in-Publication Data

Salzmann, Mary Elizabeth, 1968- author.
  Camera / Mary Elizabeth Salzmann ; consulting editor, Diane Craig, M.A./Reading Specialist.
    pages cm. -- (Amazing inventions)
  Audience: Grades PreK-3
  ISBN 978-1-62403-709-2
1. Cameras--Juvenile literature. 2. Inventions--History--Juvenile literature. I. Title.
  TR250.S24 2016
  771.3--dc23
            2014045326

SandCastle™ Level: Fluent

SandCastle™ books are created by a team of professional educators, reading specialists, and content developers around five essential components—phonemic awareness, phonics, vocabulary, text comprehension, and fluency—to assist young readers as they develop reading skills and strategies and increase their general knowledge. All books are written, reviewed, and leveled for guided reading, early reading intervention, and Accelerated Reader™ programs for use in shared, guided, and independent reading and writing activities to support a balanced approach to literacy instruction. The SandCastle™ series has four levels that correspond to early literacy development. The levels are provided to help teachers and parents select appropriate books for young readers.

EMERGING · BEGINNING · TRANSITIONAL · FLUENT

CONTENTS

ALL ABOUT CAMERAS

Cameras were invented in the 1800s.
The first ones used metal plates.

Then came **film** cameras.

The **film** gets **developed**.
It becomes a **negative**.

Pictures are printed from
the **negatives**.

They are printed on paper.

Instant cameras use special **film**.
It **develops** itself.

You can see the
picture appear.

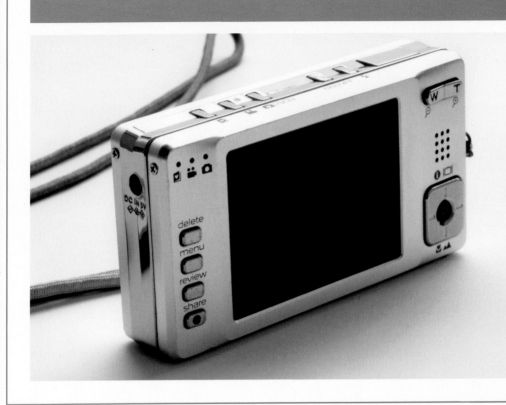

Digital cameras came out in the 1980s. They don't need **film**.

You see the pictures on a **screen**.

Digital cameras use memory cards.

The cards store the pictures.

You can put the pictures
on a computer.

You can also print them out.

Mark takes pictures of Cathy.

She is his sister.

Kim takes a picture of flowers.

They are pink and yellow.

THINK ABOUT IT

What do you like to take pictures of?

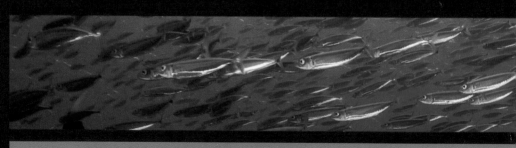

23

GLOSSARY

develop – to turn film into negatives or negatives into photographs.

digital – able to be used on a computer, or using computer technology.

film – a thin material that is used to take photographs.

negative – film that has been developed and can be used to make printed photographs.

screen – a flat surface on which information can be shown, such as a camera or computer screen.